MANDELA EFFECT

MEMORIES

Ron Deming

ISBN: 978-0-578-34506-2 (Paperback)
ISBN: 978-0-578-34505-5 (Ebook)

CONTENTS

Chapter 1: Mandela Effect 1

Chapter 2: Mandela Substitutions 21

Chapter 3: Mandela Shifts 39

Chapter 4: Mandela Subtractions 61

Chapter 5: Simulation Theory 81

Chapter 6: Conclusion 97

CHAPTER 1
MANDELA EFFECT

THE MANDELA EFFECT involves an ever-increasing number of occurrences where memories and reality are called into question. These occurrences involve a disconnect between what is believed based on a person's memory and what reality shows to be true. Mandela effects are also interchangeably known as quantum changes and Mandela changes. Each of these disconnections from reality typically affects a significant number of people while each person is impacted by an unsystematic set of Mandela effects.

An indicator that an aspect has experienced a Mandela change is the existence of the version that exists in our reality and an alternate version remembered by a group of people. There is a wide range of topics that are seemingly affected by this strange phenomenon including songs, movies, and company logos. The changes are typically trivial details that don't have an impact on people that have not noticed the change. People that have noticed a change have reactions ranging from denial to a stubborn insistence that the aspect has somehow changed.

The namesake for the Mandela effect is the former South African president, Nelson Mandela. This term was first coined by Fiona Broome, who (falsely) thought that Nelson Mandela's death occurred in the 1980s while he was still in prison. It became noteworthy enough to put a name to this phenomenon because she discovered other people at a conference also remembered Nelson Mandela's death in the same way. In reality Nelson Mandela survived his time in prison, became president in 1994, and died in 2013. People affected by this Mandela effect even remember news coverage of his death including a speech given by his wife. What is remarkable about this case is that this group is over twenty years off the mark when comparing their memory to reality. This example is an outlier given how the difference between Nelson Mandela's death happening in the 1980s and 2013 would have had a noticeable impact on the recent history of South America.

The prevailing explanation used for explaining the memories tied to the Mandela effect centers around the limitations of our brains. This is a great counter to any idea reliant on a person's memory given it's a plausible explanation and most people can relate to this acute shortcoming. Many memories tied to Mandela changes come from aspects people have not paid much attention to since their childhood. This further puts the shortcomings of memory into focus because childhood memories are particularly susceptible to alterations. People believing Mandela effects are caused by faulty memories which are sometimes referred to as "skeptics" and "debunkers" of alternate explanations.

Alternate explanations are understandably compared to the logical explanation of people misremembering a trivial detail. The simplest explanation is often the preferred answer to a problem, so it is not surprising that so many people gravitate towards this explanation. There is also an abundance of reliable studies showing just how weak our memories truly are.

A key point in favor of quantum effects being caused by the limitations of human brains is the existence and pervasiveness of false memories. False memories are inaccurate recollections caused by a variety of reasons such as implanted ideas and subconsciously overwriting memories that conflict with ideas shared within a peer group. The existence of false memories is helpful since people are social beings with brains that actively conform to environmental influences. The consistency and solidarity provided by false memories is preferrable to conflicting ideas coexisting in a person's mind. The high level of confidence tied to false memories makes them more difficult to recognize and accept as incorrect.

It's unfortunate since people are less likely to do research and consider the validity of opposing ideas when their memory is supported by a high level of confidence. Confronting someone about potential false memories they are already comfortable with, such as those associated with Mandela effects, is an uphill battle.

False memories are made possible in part

because our brains store bits of information with a proximity-based organizational method reliant on similarities. As memory fades due to disuse, it's possible for these similar memories to blend together. Newly blended ideas could then overwrite the related weaker memories and might feel like a clearer memory due to being created more recently. People with weak memories of the same idea could have a similar blending of ideas through an external source such as leading questions sometimes used in Mandela quizzes. This could lead to a group of people experiencing a shared memory with more clarity than would be expected for ideas they have not accessed lately. A possible signal that this type of overwriting of memories has occurred is a memory from childhood associated with a quantum change having a high level of clarity for no apparent reason.

The likelihood of weak memories blending together in this manner is increased because memories are reconstructed each time they're accessed. A memory gets stronger the more often it's accessed because the brain has more practice reconstructing that idea. This's why studying helps and the reason people can become an expert in a given field after years of reconstructing ideas about the same topic. It stands to reason that the converse is also true, which means a memory becomes weaker if it is not important enough to be accessed with regularity. This means it's not a coincidence for Mandela effects to be more often associated with ideas that are not reconstructed on a regular basis. Blending of related ideas might occur if the brain determines the combination of these less accessed memories is plausible enough. Reconstructing a memory that has merged recently due to it being brought up as a Mandela change could cause a false sense of confidence in the freshly made memory.

The idea of memories becoming increasingly blurred from disuse lends itself to countermeasures used by the brain such as filling in gaps of memory with plausible replacements. This generally unobtrusive strategy for dealing with gaps in memory is accomplished using schema and stereotypes. Memories are like recreated puzzles and the brain would rather fill in a piece of this puzzle with a slightly inaccurate detail rather than have a gap. Also, the existence of reasonable replacements for aspects within memories puts less pressure on the brain to accurately store infrequently accessed information. This tradeoff of a memory's accuracy with the conservation of brain-power is especially worthwhile when the gap is associated with a trivial detail. It makes sense for people to have similar gaps in their memories because the memories associated with Mandela effects are more susceptible to having gaps. The schema and stereotypes learned in society are similar enough to potentially cause a group of people to fill in memory gaps with the same plausible replacement.

A combination of these flaws, inherent to infrequently accessed memories, make it plausible for Mandela effects to be the result of confabulation. Confabulation happens when a person's memory is replaced by a falsification that they persistently believe is correct. The confidence in the reliability of a memory can continue even when evidence clearly shows the person's recollection is incorrect. The brain's tendency toward internal consistency can work against the person experiencing confabulation when these false memories are reinforced by other people with the same misconception.

Having repetition of false information by multiple people allows the brain to confidently hold onto the cemented falsehood. The mental gymnastics a person can accomplish to maintain internal consistency about false information is impressive but also unfortunate. Confabulation might explain why groups of people confidently remember the same Mandela changes in the same way. It is possible that the importance of maintaining consistency for these false memories is enough to dismiss the contradicting data that is evident in our reality.

Memories have been contradicting reality due to the misinformation effect long before the Mandela effect was coined. It would be fair to attribute a mixture of factors, including suggestibility and misattribution of memory, to the formation and spread of quantum changes. The misinformation effect has been proven to impact people in important scenarios such as while giving testimony in court. Lawyers are supposed to avoid asking leading questions because this can influence the memory that the witness is accessing.

Trivial information (such as movie lines and music lyrics) is likely to be more susceptible to change due to suggestibility and misattribution of memory rather than memories accessed during witness testimony. Furthermore, misleading information responsible for the misinformation effect can enter the equation at any point in the process of intentionally or unintentionally spreading falsehoods. Repetition of misinformation combined with reinforcement through confirmation bias helps explain how it is possible for memories associated with Mandela changes to have a high level of confidence.

It is important to accept that people can concurrently believe their memory is flawed and believe Mandela effects are not always caused by misremembering details. For example, my memory is undeniably flawed, which helped me see the appeal of misremembrance as an explanation for Mandela changes. I would have continued to agree with the idea of quantum changes being caused by flawed memories if I hadn't found examples that I could not rationalize away.

This lack of explanatory consistency drove me to dive deeper into the topic and find ways to rationalize these examples or explore viable alternatives. When rationalizing ultimately failed for a couple examples I was exploring, it opened the door for taking the idea of another explanation seriously, even if it ended up not being provable. It is very likely that some ideas attributed to the Mandela effect are actually caused by reasons such as misremembrance, cognitive dissonance, and misconceptions. If a single example is unexplainable through these types of reasons, then it opens up some interesting possibilities.

The number of possible ways to misremember and/or miscommunicate a detail makes it remarkable that each alternate memory attributed to a Mandela change is remembered the same way. This distinct lack of variety is peculiar given each person has at least slightly different information to pull from when the brain chooses an appropriate replacement for weak memories and/or gaps. This problem is avoided if an alternate version of a seemingly changed aspect is an example of a widely spread instance of miscommunication.

There would likely still be at least some variation if miscommunication is involved, given how shared information has a tendency to change due to further instances of miscommunication.

A prime example of this is the telephone

game, which is intended to demonstrate how easy it is for miscommunication to happen and the number of variations that can emerge within a short time period. If misremembrance and/or miscommunication is the cause of Mandela effects, then it makes more sense for multiple groups to exist for each Mandela change based on which variation of the aspect they remember.

Another factor that points toward the viability of an alternative explanation is how this is a relatively new phenomenon, even though people have had fallible memories for thousands of years. It is true that we now have technology which provides unprecedented methods of connectivity and preservation of information. However, access to forms of communication, such as the internet, does not adequately explain the newness of this phenomenon. In fact, they existed for decades before the Mandela effect was even discovered.

Misconceptions have been known about for a long time, so an even more disconcerting type of mismatch between memory and reality is unlikely to go unnoticed for thousands of years. A collective misremembering on the scale of Mandela changes would likely be an ancient and widely known phenomenon if poor memory is responsible for this irregularity. It is not just the coining of the concept that is new, given people's recent discovery of the term after researching these disconcerting mismatches between their memory and reality.

The existence of a multitude of parallel universes is another common explanation for the emergence of Mandela changes. The explanatory power of this option relies on the purported ability to have coexisting parallel universes that are only slightly different from each other. If the existence of these coexisting universes is possible, then it would explain how a shift in consciousness between two parallel universes only results in minor discrepancies.

This book will focus on the method for generating universes which is reliant on quantum mechanics because it is great at explaining the existence of parallel universes that differ slightly. Details being slightly different in each parallel reality adequately explains how some people are affected by quantum changes, while others remember the detail correctly. The people that remember the detail correctly are likely from a universe in which the detail is the same or they are in their original universe. The existence of a multiverse where a person's consciousness can shift between parallel universes could be a new development, which would explain why it is a relatively new concept.

The existence of residue is a problem regardless of whether the emergence of Mandela changes is caused by the fallibility of memories or mobility of consciousness in a multiverse. Mandela effect residue is an altered representation of an aspect such as a meme or a parody. Residue is important because it matches the alternate version of an aspect that has seemingly changed. A group remembering an aspect as portrayed by residue can use this as evidence that a change has occurred.

On the other hand, residue can be used to show the extensive reach of misremembrance or explain where the idea behind the alternate version originated. The existence of residue is problematic for explaining the Mandela effect through misremembrance because it provides evidence that another explanation is viable. Having residue matching the version of an aspect from a person's original parallel universe stretches the bounds of a believable coincidence. This is because the number of possible deviations for a given aspect is vast.

The way in which similar parallel universes are plausibly formed is through the collapse of wave functions in each perpetually branching universe. The collapse of a wave function is known as the point at which wave functions are no longer in a state of superposition. Particles are typically in superposition, which is a counterintuitive state involving attributes such as location being represented by a range of probabilistic outcomes rather than a definite value. A particle is essentially encompassing all outcomes at the same time while it is in the state of superposition. The process for branching universes involves all possible outcomes of a wave function collapse happening with each result branching into a new parallel universe. There is a considerable number of extremely similar parallel universes, if this how the universes are formed, because a single wave function collapse is not particularly impactful. This dizzying number of parallel universes explains why people with a shifted consciousness have alternate memories while most details match their original universe.

The inescapable conclusion that particles exist in a state of superposition has been demonstrated repeatedly through the double slit experiment. A single particle sent toward the double slit exhibits a probabilistic tendency by creating an interference pattern on the measuring apparatus placed beyond the two slits. The lone particle is able to create an interference pattern because the range of possible paths includes both slits.

It is evident that the existence of probabilistic outcomes for each slit happening at the same time causes possible outcomes from each slit to interfere with each other. This would not be possible if each particle did not behave like a wave of probable locations, rather than existing in a state of definite attributes. The ability to concurrently encompass every probable outcome before measurement occurs is not unique to lone particles. An interference pattern has also been demonstrated when a single atom or molecule is used during double slit experiments.

It is apparent that the reason a particle does not remain in superposition indefinitely is the ability to measure various attributes of each particle. An alternate possibility involves a collapse happening when a particle interacts with a factor in its environment capable of causing decoherence. This alternate explanation for wave function collapse is untenable given the particles in a star remain in superposition for billions of years as evidenced by them continually emitting light. The fusion reactions within a star responsible for emitting light is dependent on particles remaining in superposition so that quantum tunneling is still possible.

Fusion reactions would not be possible if the particles were already in a state of definite characteristics rather than having a small chance of accomplishing quantum tunneling. If constant interactions in a star over the span of billions of years is not enough to cause decoherence, then it is unlikely this alternate explanation for wave function collapse is better than the idea of measurements being the determining factor.

An example closer to home that also demonstrates the lack of explanatory power for decoherence is the interactions during photosynthesis. The first step of photosynthesis involves an electromagnetic interaction between photons and the electrons found in chlorophyll, which results in a transfer of energy to the electron. There is a mazelike path the excited electron must take within the span of one nanosecond so that the energy is stored safely by the plant in the reaction center. It is likely the only reason photosynthesis happens with nearly 100% efficiency, despite the convoluted maze the excited electron must navigate in a ridiculously short time period, is by remaining in superposition.

The packet of energy would not reach the correct destination if the electron's interaction with the photon or interactions during its journey to the reaction center were sufficient for collapsing its wave function. If the messy environment within a leaf is not enough to cause wave functions to collapse, then the idea of decoherence loses its explanatory power for what is documented during the double slit experiment.

The delayed-choice quantum eraser experiment provides another piece of the puzzle regarding determining the viability of branching universes through wave-function collapses. This experiment adds extra features to the double slit experiment such as a crystal for creating entangled pairs of particles, multiple forms of measurement, and the loss of results from some measurements. One of the entangled particles is measured at a screen without any attempts to measure the which-path data. This means that all these particles should show an interference pattern.

However, the outcome of the particle measured at the screen is determined by what happens to its entangled twin, which has a delayed measurement of its which-path data. This means the entangled particles are measured at two different points in time and the measurement of the which-path data happens after the screen has made a measurement. The interesting finding from this experiment is that a particle's pattern on the screen is determined by whether the which-path data of its entangled twin is measured.

The key feature that makes the different results on the screen meaningful for determining the viability of branching universes is the ability to have an intentional loss of which-path data for the delayed measurement. A fascinating outcome is an interference pattern emerging when the which-path data of the delayed measurement is not recorded while an interference pattern does not emerge on the screen when the which-path data of delayed measurement is recorded. If the first measurement and/or interaction at the screen determined the overall outcome, then all results would become an interference pattern because the wave-function for its entangled twin would collapse before the delayed measurement happened.

If the delayed measurement of the entangled particle was sufficient for making the interference pattern on the screen disappear, then it should not matter if the result of the delayed measurement is recorded. The intentional loss of which-path data for a delayed measurement (resulting in an interference pattern on the screen) shows that the collapse of a wave function is dependent on whether the result is recorded.

The branching of parallel universes has a problem with timing if the mechanism has a consistent process. It is important to try and determine when the multiple outcomes associated with the multiverse are no longer possible outcomes in our own universe due to already branching into their own universes. There is a problem with the timing of branching if parallel universes (by means of wave function) collapse if branching occurs before a measurement happens.

The existence of wave functions would effectively be unknown if all possible outcomes represented by the wave function branched into isolated universes before interference could occur. If branching happens during an interaction and/or measurement, then multiple results would be impossible during the delayed-choice quantum eraser because the branching would happen before the delayed measurement occurred. If two interactions and/or measurements were sufficient for the branching of universes, then different results would not be observable on the screen, depending on whether the information is recorded or lost. This likely means that the branching of parallel universes is inconsistent or involves a mechanism with increased complexity.

CHAPTER 2
MANDELA SUBSTITUTIONS

THERE ARE AT least three different types of quantum changes. The one that will be covered in this chapter is Mandela substitutions. Substitutions include the most trivial of changes, such as a word being spelled differently, a letter in a word being replaced, and words in a movie or song being different. Arguments about these quantum changes are difficult to prove on either side of the argument between misremembrance and people thinking a change has occurred since the current and alternate version are extremely interchangeable.

These are excellent examples to use when demonstrating the plausibility of memory playing a role in the emergence of Mandela changes because people can easily relate to misremembering this type of information. People arguing from the stance of thinking a change has occurred is typically at a disadvantage when dealing with substitutions given how common misquotes and misspellings are. It is still an important category to recognize because they are the most abundant type of Mandela effect to emerge. The following Mandela substitutions are a small sample compared to the overall number of examples out there.

Forrest Gump is a memorable movie that won six Academy Awards, three Golden Globe Awards, six Saturn Awards, and a slew of other awards. An iconic line from Tom Hank's portrayal of Forrest Gump is "My mom always said life was like a box of chocolates. You never know what you're gonna get." The alternate version some people remember is "Life is like a box of chocolates. You never know what you're gonna get." Having the word "was" in the quote makes sense in terms of explaining the discrepancy through misremembrance given that Forrest might be quoting what his mama used to say.

The fact that life continues to be like a box of chocolates is probably not grasped by the character because of his low IQ. There is arguably some residue for the prior existence of the quote having "is" instead of "was" including the misquoting of the iconic line on the box of the VHS and DVD. It is surprising this mistake was not fixed on the DVD box even though it released years after the VHS copy.

Oscar Mayer is a company well known for bologna, hot dogs, and other meats. The spelling of Oscar Mayer should be familiar to many people given their catchy songs that get people to sing the name and even spell the entire name. There is a divide between people remembering the current name of Oscar Mayer and those who remember the company being called Oscar Meyer. One point in favor of people remembering incorrectly is the pronunciation of the letter 'a' in Mayer not being a long vowel sound.

There is an 'e' in the second half of the name, so this is a likely replacement if a person's memory of the name is weak. A possible piece of residue for the alternate version of the company's name is a category on an episode of Jeopardy from April 27, 2005, that used the name "Oscar Meyer". It is interesting that none of the people involved in creating the category and/or the accompanying questions happened to notice the well-known company's name was spelled incorrectly.

Let's Call the Whole Thing Off is a song from 1937 where comparisons are made between British and American English accents. Some lyrics from the song use "like" for comparisons while other lyrics use "say". A part of this song that has stood the test of time is "You like potato and I like *potahto.* You like tomato and I like *tomahto*". The alternate memory for this verse involves "say" being used instead of "like". People remembering "say" instead of "like" might be mentally fixing the song, so it makes more sense. The word "like" makes it seem like the person was given options and chose the version they preferred; however, this is not normally the case.

Pronunciations are typically learned, and people continue using the version they are familiar with. There is seemingly a mismatch in the song when considering the consistency for comparing pronunciations and with the variety used when singing "like" instead of "say".

The Berenstain Bears are popular

characters that have appeared in books, a television series, and video games. The wide-reaching popularity has not stopped many people from having an alternate memory of the characters being known as the Berenstein Bears. It makes sense for people to misremember the name as Berenstein instead of many other possible alternatives because "-stein" is more commonly used as a suffix in names. Discrepancies in peoples' memory are also more likely for an example such as the Berenstain Bears because many people have not had exposure to the name since their own childhood.

Some possible residue for this change exists in the form of the name being mispronounced in a TV commercial from 1994 that promoted the Sega Club. No one happened to correct this mistake at any point in the process of creating the commercial even though there is no mistaking that he said "Berenstein" instead of "Berenstain". This mistake making it into the final version of the commercial would make more sense if the characters were not so well known around this time.

Snow White is a classic fairy tale that Disney made into an animated film in 1937.

One of the best-known quotes from this movie is "Magic Mirror on the wall, who is the fairest one of all?" A group of people remember the evil queen saying "Mirror, mirror on the wall, who is the fairest one of all?" There are many ways this misquote could have been attributed to the film, including the wording in the original Brothers Grimm tale being "Mirror, mirror".

The quote "Mirror, mirror" is so commonly attributed to the 1937 film that it is even misquoted on Disney-branded merchandise. Parodies and reenactments of this scene consistently misquote the line as "Mirror, mirror on the wall". You can hear the line misquoted in *Shrek, The Fresh Prince of Bel Air, The Simpsons,* and other movies and TV shows. The sheer number of times this line is seemingly misquoted is strange enough to raise questions of whether the line from the original movie was changed somehow.

Even the Bible is not immune to apparent changes. Various versions of Isaiah 11:6 mention a wolf living with a lamb, which is great imagery for a peaceful time to come. A common mistake is made by switching the wolf for a lion in this verse. The verse having wolf instead of lion makes more sense given that wolves are natural predators of sheep. The current version works well as imagery for a peaceful time because a shepherd would not be needed if the wolf lives with the lamb rather than trying to eat it. However, the Bible is a popular book to read, memorize, and create imagery for, which makes it more difficult to imagine so many people depicting this verse incorrectly. It is expected for some people to make this mistake, but a vast majority of imagery available for this verse shows a lion instead of a wolf.

"Objects in mirror are closer than they appear" is a required safety warning on side mirrors and has been seen repeatedly by millions of people over the years. A significant group of people remember an alternate version that says, "may be" instead of "are". The warning changes from a certainty to an uncertainty, which is unusual because intent and/or meaning are generally maintained to a greater degree by the alternate version.

It is possible that people are conflating this warning with the many other warnings that say "may result". An interesting example of residue for this possible change is David Letterman's top 10 list from February 13, 2001. The top ten list of things that sound cool when spoken by James Earl Jones included "Objects in mirror may be closer than they appear" at number nine. The inclusion in the top 10 list could be evidence of a change or just reinforce how widespread this potential mix-up is.

Scary Movie is known for its humorous parodies based on a variety of different movies. One exception is the copy and paste of a well-known line from the movie *The Sixth Sense*. "I see dead people" is said in *Scary Movie* and is even displayed on the movie's poster. A group of people remember the line as "I see white people" for the poster, trailer, and movie. The possible false memory might originate from *Undercover Brother*, which is a comedy where a character humorously says, "I see white people".

Arguably, the evidence for a change is just how out of place the current version is. Using "I see white people" in the movie would have made a funny scene, which would match the other funny scenes within the movie. "I see dead people" also does not fit the tone of the movie. Its inclusion on the movie's poster doesn't make sense as it gives the impression that the movie is blatantly ripping off other movies rather than its actual approach of parodying scary movies.

Scary Movie 2 parodies supernatural movies such as *The Haunting, Poltergeist, The Exorcist,* and *The Rocky Horror Picture Show*. There is a funny scene where a character named Dwight Hartman would rather fall to his death than to take the character of Hanson's little hand with stubby fingers. Dwight asks for Hanson's other hand, but Hanson replies, "My other hand isn't strong enough. You take my little hand". Some people remember Hanson saying, "Take my strong hand". A false memory could easily be to blame for this alternate version since Hanson refers to his smaller hand as his "strong hand" earlier in the movie.

Again, there is a distinct lack of consistency within the movie since the character abruptly switches from referring to the strength of his hands to the size of his hands. There are obvious hints in the movie pointing to the character's ignorance of his left hand being different, so abandoning the schtick in this manner is baffling. Possible residue also exists in the form of memes using "take my strong hand" instead of "little hand".

The Lone Ranger is a fictional masked hero that has been portrayed in a radio series, television show, books, and movies. "Hi-yo, Silver, away!" is the Lone Ranger's catchphrase and has been widely known to people over the past decades. This catchphrase is surprising to the many people remembering the quote as "Hi-ho, Silver, away!". It is possible that memories of the Lone Ranger's catchphrase have blended with memories of "Heigh-Ho" being sung by the seven dwarfs in *Snow White*.

Having such a minor difference between the current version and alternate memory can also contribute to uncertainty about which version is correct. It is certain that the alternate version is used during the projector scene in *Ace Ventura: When Nature Calls,* the Saleen S7 scene in *Bruce Almighty,* and *The Lone Ranger* from 2013. The alternate version showing up in a movie based on the character by the same name is especially awkward.

Kellogg's Froot Loops is a widely recognized brand of cereal that is sold in many countries and has existed since 1963. The alternate memory for the name of this colorful cereal is Fruit Loops. It makes sense that some people remember the name as Fruit Loops since it is fruit flavored. It also makes sense for the double "o" in both words since this incorporates the product itself into the logo consistently as a replacement for vowels. Residue for the alternate version might exist in Van Halen's 1982 World Tour rider, which famously bans brown M&Ms from the band's dressing room. Fruit loops is listed as one of the possible choices for cereals served at 8:30 a.m. on each day of a scheduled performance as outlined on page 36 of the rider. This rider is extremely detail oriented, so it is surprising that an obvious spelling mistake slipped through to the final version.

Star Wars: Episode V – The Empire Strikes Back has one of one of the most famous and shocking quotes in cinema history, which is widely remembered as "Luke, I am your father." The actual version of this quote is "No, I am your father." The shock factor involved with this revelation might have played a role in people potentially misremembering the line. It also makes sense to replace "No" with "Luke" when repeating it to other people because it makes the quote unambiguous. A strong piece of possible residue exists in the form of James Earl Jones's distinctive voice saying the alternate version of this line. This can be heard when pressing a button on the Hallmark ornament of Darth Vader from 2005. If this is actual residue, then it is incredible because somehow this recording of the alternate line did not change while the current version of the line is heard in every copy of the movie.

Peanut butter is a common pantry staple with some standout brands including Jif, Skippy, and Peter Pan. However, a group of people remember the leading peanut butter brand as Jiffy. Some people even remember a shift from Jiffy to Jiff before becoming Jif. This is a multi-step change instead of three different versions of the peanut butter since these people distinctly remember all three versions existing at different times. Brand names for peanut butter are possibly trivial enough for the brain to combine Skippy peanut butter and Jif peanut butter into Jiffy peanut butter. Out of the numerous possible pieces of residue for the alternate name of this peanut butter, the definitions for the word "jiffy" on Urban Dictionary won out. Two of the definitions refer to peanut butter in the description of the term. This is interesting since the site uses groups of people when publishing definitions, yet none of them caught the incorrect connection being made in two separate definitions of the same word.

A popular cartoon many people have watched over the years is *Looney Tunes*. This might look wrong to you if you are part of the group that remembers the show being called *Looney Toons*. It is not a stretch of the imagination to suppose people remember this incorrectly due to the show being a cartoon rather than a music performance. The words "tune" and "toon" sounding the same is not helpful in terms of remembering the spelling correctly. A strange disconnect is seen when comparing the names of two cartoons within the same cartoon universe. *Tiny Toon Adventures* uses a different spelling than its predecessor, even though characters from this show are going to school in order to become the next generation of *Looney Tunes*. This would be more understandable to attribute to misremembrance if *Tiny Toon Adventures* was a rip-off of the original, but that is not the case.

Field of Dreams is a well-known movie that was nominated for three Academy

Awards. An important scene involves Ray Kinsella hearing a voice whisper, "If you build it, he will come." A widely remembered alternate version of the line is "If you build it, they will come." People could easily misremember this aspect of the quote since the use of "he" does not make much sense in the context of the movie. The people that are apparently misremembering this quote might have subconsciously fixed this inconsistency from the movie by replacing "he" with "they".

Multiple players show up and a crowd of spectators is made up of more than one person, which could further cement the incorrect version of the quote into peoples' memory. A conceivable piece of residue is found in a similar scenario from *Wayne's World 2*, in which the character is told, "If you build it, they will come".

Sally Field won an Academy Award for Best Actress in a Leading Role for her role in *Places in the Heart*. "I can't deny the fact that you like me. Right now, you like me!" is a memorable line from her Oscar acceptance speech in 1985. A sizable group of people remember an alternate version of this line in which she says, "You like me, you really like me!"

Sally Field says, "Let's see which one you like. You really, really like!" when she announced the Best Actor during the 1986 Oscars. These two quotes were told in a similar context, so it makes sense for memories of the two quotes to possibly combine into the alternate version. It could be argued that the quote from 1986 is residue for the alternate version of her own acceptance speech. Another possible piece of residue is heard when "You love me, you really love me!" is used as a mock acceptance speech in the movie *The Mask*.

Mister Rogers' Neighborhood is one of the longest-running children's television series and has a widely known opening theme called "Won't You Be My Neighbor?" Mister Rogers started each episode by walking through the door and singing "It's a beautiful day in this neighborhood." A group of people remember Mister Rogers being more inclusive by singing "It's a beautiful day in the neighborhood." False memories could be to blame given the involvement of childhood memories and other versions using "the" instead of "this" such as the theme song for *Daniel Tiger's Neighborhood*.

A Beautiful Day in the Neighborhood is a movie based on actual events in Fred Roger's life, which makes the movie title's alteration of the line disconcerting. A blatant mistake in the title is difficult to overlook because each person involved in the production process should know the movie's title. It would have been a fast and easy fix if a single person noticed the substitution and mentioned the mistake.

The Silence of the Lambs is a psychological horror movie from 1991 that is known as one of the best and most influential films. Anthony Hopkins plays the cannibalistic serial killer Hannibal Lecter and Jodie Foster portrays a student from the FBI Academy known as Clarice Starling. Hannibal Lecter famously said, "Hello, Clarice" when Clarice interviewed the serial killer for the first time. The problem with this is he actually quietly said, "Good morning" instead of "Hello, Clarice".

Hannibal Lecter doesn't actually say this phrase until the trailer of *Hannibal* in 2001, which is a possible source for misremembering what was said during their original meeting. However, this does not explain parodies that emerged between the release of the two films such as Ernie 'Chip' Douglas saying it in *The Cable Guy*, which released in 1996. It is unmistakable where the inspiration for this parody came from given Jim Carrey's character says, "Silence of the lambs. Hello, Clarice. It's good to see you again."

The importance of using residue from movies and television shows is linked to the number of people involved with these types of projects. Many examples of residue have a higher level of uncertainty because they involve one person's memory, or a project completed by a small group. The appropriateness of attributing false memories to an alternate version is plausibly proportional to the number of people involved.

The likelihood of false memories being involved with a piece of residue should decrease as the number of people exposed to this aspect of the project increases. If the current version of a given aspect existed when the scene was originally brainstormed, performed, and edited, then the mistake had a high chance of being fixed. It is outside the bounds of reasonable coincidences for every person involved with a large project to have the exact same false memory of a given aspect. Therefore, the feasibility of Mandela effects is strengthened by residue persisting in movies and other undertakings that involve a sizable group of people.

CHAPTER 3
MANDELA SHIFTS

THE SECOND TYPE of quantum change is a Mandela shift, which involves a range of possible aspects beyond the scope of words changing. Rationalizing false memories associated with these more extensive changes can become problematic because there is more room for reasonable doubt. Misremembering a single word in an iconic movie in the same way as many other people is understandable because the possible replacements are somewhat limited by the context of the line and overall scene.

Remembering the exact same details for the more complex aspects associated with Mandela shifts is intriguing because there are more possible combinations involved with the formation of a false memory. However, it is not impossible for shifts to be caused by multiple people accidentally forming the same alternate version and/or spreading an incorrect description widely enough to form a group with the same false memory. The balance of power between those purporting misremembrance and those believing a change has occurred is on more equal footing for Mandela shifts.

Footage of President John F. Kennedy's assassination on November 22, 1963, has been viewed and analyzed by many people over the years. The current footage of this historical event clearly shows a total of six people in the vehicle. Some people remember an alternate version in which there were only four seats and people in the car. People watching the footage are typically focusing on the assassination of JFK, so it would be easy for them to forget or not notice an extra set of people in the car. Possible residue for JFK being shot in a car with four seats is the model displayed at Historic Auto Attractions in Roscoe, Illinois. Other museum exhibits use a version of the car with six seats. Somehow, none of the people involved with the display at Historic Auto Attractions noticed this inaccuracy. The inconsistency in car models used in museum exhibits introduces a modicum of uncertainty about whether a change has occurred.

Many of the characters from *Alice in Wonderland* are memorable, particuarly Tweedledum and Tweedledee. The movie adaptation from 1951 depicts these characters with rounded torsos, clothes with mismatched colors, and a red hat with a small flag sticking out the top. A group of people remembers both characters looking the same except for their hats being multicolored with a propeller sticking out the top. The hats worn by Tweedledum and Tweedledee are sort of reminiscent of propeller hats and the flags rotate like propellers do.

This association mixed with a weak memory of their hats could result in memories of the flags being replaced by propellers. It makes sense for people to misremember the hats as being multicolored because the rest of their outfit makes use of multiple colors. The shared memory of multicolored hats with propellers has existed long enough for this combination of aspects to exist for various costumes and depictions. Although, these costumes might be residue of a change along with the depiction of Tweedledee and

Tweedledum found in *The Simpsons* season 28 episode 11.

See-Threepio (C-3PO) is an oblivious protocol droid found in various *Star Wars* novels, television shows, comics, and the *Star Wars* movie trilogies. One of C3PO's features that helps distinguish him from similar protocol droids is the silver coloring of his lower right leg and foot. This is somewhat troubling for people remembering his lower half as typically being mono-colored. This portion of C3PO's body is frequently blocked from view, difficult to see due to background colors, or seen in bad lighting. These factors paired with a memory of gold coloring for most of his body could combine into a false memory of both feet and legs being mono-colored.

The lack of silver on C-3PO's leg is seen in comic books, action figures, stickers, and the 1985 animated television series *Star Wars: Droids: The Adventures of R2-D2 and C-3PO*. It is strange for a show focused on C-3PO's adventures to overlook this detail if the coloring of his lower right leg has not changed.

E.T. the Extra-Terrestrial is a well-known film about E.T. being stranded on Earth and centers around a bond he forms with a child named Elliott. In one scene, E.T. is learning words to let the children know he wants to contact his fellow aliens. He conveys this message by saying, "E.T. home phone" followed by both kids and E.T. saying, "E.T. phone home". Some people remember E.T. consistently saying, "E.T. phone home" instead of him saying "E.T. home phone" the first time.

A false memory of this line could understandably form given that "E.T. home phone" is said once while "E.T. phone home" is said six times in that scene alone. However, there is an intriguing segment of the movie's first official trailer in which "E.T. phone home" is heard instead of "E.T. home phone". We hear "E.T. phone home" while the shadow of E.T.'s hand is on Elliott's face, which fits the memory of E.T. saying the same line consistently.

Uncle Sam is a recognizable personification of the United States' federal government and his current features date back to World War I. The original version of his hat has a white crown and a sizeable blue band with prominent, white five-pointed stars. The alternate memory of this hat includes vertical red stripes on the crown, which gives the hat a strong connection to the American flag. The blue band with white stars on the current version is reminiscent of the American flag, so people could straightforwardly incorporate red stripes into their memories of Uncle Sam's hat.

The potential residue for the alternate version of Uncle Sam's hat is overwhelming in its abundance. For example, the alternate version is used by Apollo Creed during his entrance to the title match in *Rocky*. Representations of the original version are more difficult to find than the alternate version, which is unusual for Mandela changes. There is a plausible reason for the abundance of residue for this peculiarity, which is covered in chapter five.

The Thinker is a widely recognized statue by Auguste Rodin that has been used to represent philosophy and has been recreated numerous times. The first known iteration of this possible change associated with the statue involved its fist moving from its forehead to under its chin. It makes sense for memories to become mixed up for the placement of the statue's fist given that both poses characterize a person that is thinking. What doesn't make as much sense is for people to mix up the pose when they are mimicking the statue's pose while standing next to *The Thinker*.

That is exactly what is seen in pictures where an individual or a group of people put their fist to their forehead even though the statue has a different pose right next to them. It makes sense for people to be quite aware of the correct pose in the presence of the actual statue and the photographer doesn't even seem to notice a discrepancy.

The version of the statue posed with his fist to his forehead and with the one with his fist under his chin are both incorrect. The current version of *The Thinker* clearly shows the statue's hand under its chin with an open hand. The difference between an open hand under the chin and a fist are subtle enough to explain the possible emergence of false memories.

What is so interesting about *The Thinker* is the possibility that it has undergone two separate Mandela changes. Somehow, people in pictures managed to get the head and chin mixed up while also failing to notice the difference between a fist and an open hand. Also, there is a big difference between memories becoming distorted after years of not being accessed and the fresh memory of the people visiting and posing next to the actual statue. *The Thinker* might be a critical piece of the puzzle since the statue seemingly changed multiple times while residue from pictures did not shift accordingly.

Tutankhamun aka *"King Tut"* is well-known for being a young pharaoh of Egypt and for artifacts such as his golden mask that were found in his well-preserved tomb. Ancient Egypt is a popular topic of study and King Tut's golden mask is a frequently used artifact for portraying Egypt's rich history. King Tut's golden mask is a death mask with Tutankhamun's likeness and includes a prominent vulture and cobra on the forehead. Some people remember the mask being the same design except for having a lone cobra rather than two animals as seen on the actual version. It is possible the cobra is more memorable to people, which would explain how people have seemingly forgotten about the vulture on the mask. One possible piece of residue is the headgear worn by King Tut in the aptly named television miniseries called *Tut.* The cobra is used as a visual cue for the audience, which makes the lack of a vulture worth noting.

Pikachu is one of the most recognizable species from the *Pokémon* franchise due to being a primary mascot as well as appearing in various video games, movies, and the animated series. Pikachu is mostly yellow with a red circle on each cheek and two brown stripes on its back. It also has a brown section at the base of its lightning bolt shaped tail and the tips of its ears are black. A group of people remember the mouse-like Pokémon having a black section at the end of its tail instead of having a brown section at the base of its tail. Misremembrance could understandably happen if people mentally add black to the end of the tail to complement the black tips of its ears and/or incorporate the black tail of Pichu into the appearance of Pikachu. Possible residue for this change is seen in *The Simpsons* season 24 episode 4, in which Maggie's counterpart has Pikachu's distinctive, black-tipped tail and ears while also not having a brown base for the tail.

The *Mona Lisa* is a masterpiece by Leonardo da Vinci that is one of the most valuable, best known, and most visited paintings in the world. The current version shows a smirking lady with curly hair sitting upright in an armchair in front of an imaginary landscape. The alternate version is remembered as having an ambiguous smile unlike the quite obvious smirk seen on the current version. The perpetuation of doubt about the *Mona Lisa*'s smile could cause memories to conform to this idea, which would cause people to remember the smile as more ambiguous than it really is.

The alternate version is seen in a picture from *The Da Vinci Code* with Tom Hanks and Audrey Tautou standing in front of the painting while mimicking the Mona Lisa's lack of an obvious smile. It is strange that the replica was able to reproduce the image so well except for a deviation for the aspect that makes the painting so well known.

The Statue of Liberty is an iconic torch-wielding copper statue based on the Roman goddess of liberty that France gifted to the United States in 1886. This statue is a New York City landmark and a national monument that is currently located on Liberty Island and is visited by millions of people each year. A group of people have an alternate memory in which the Statue of Liberty was located on Ellis Island. The alternate version of the statue's location could stem from the nearly twelve million immigrants processed at the immigration station on Ellis Island. This number of immigrants closely ties the idea of liberty to Ellis Island even though the Statue of Liberty is located on another island. A piece of possible residue for the statue being on Ellis Island is found on the 1986 Statue of Liberty commemorative silver dollar because the coin says Ellis Island on it. This is strange because the coin is clearly commemorating the statue rather than the concept of liberty.

Ed McMahon is well-known for being a sidekick on *The Tonight Show Starring Johnny Carson,* hosting *Star Search,* and appearing in commercials and movies. He was also the original spokesperson for *American Family Publishers,* which sold magazine subscriptions and held sweepstakes for large amounts of money. A group of people remembers Ed McMahon working as a spokesperson for a competing company known as *Publishers Clearing House.* He is also mistakenly remembered for visiting the sweepstakes winner's house with a massive check, which is strange since he also didn't perform this role for American Family Publishers. It is not a stretch of the imagination for people to conflate a well-known sweepstakes spokesperson with a well-known company for sweepstakes. Possible residue for this example includes an episode of *Late Night with David Letterman* in which Johnny Carson presents an oversized check to Letterman. Carson mentions Ed McMahon repeatedly in connection to the check and it clearly says Publishers Clearing House on the check.

Poppin' Fresh aka, *the Pillsbury Doughboy* is well-known as Pillsbury's mascot and has been seen in more than six hundred commercials over the years. This iconic character is widely recognized by his dough-like body, chef's hat, blue eyes, white neckerchief, and the giggle he does when poked in the stomach. The variation in the Pillsbury Doughboy's appearance that is remembered by a group of people centers around his neckerchief being blue instead of white. A memory that could plausibly conflate with the color of his neckerchief is the blue sailor's collar seen around the neck of the Stay-Puft Marshmallow Man from *Ghostbusters*. Possible residue includes The Pillsbury Doughboy having a blue neckerchief while Mr. Burns hallucinates in *The Simpsons* season 7 episode 12. Poppin' Fresh can also be seen wearing a blue neckerchief before he is squashed by Lois in *Family Guy* season 1 episode 7. It is interesting that people working on these two shows seemingly misremembered this iconic character in the same way.

Cruella De Vil is an over-the-top villain known for her desire to kill dalmatian puppies in order to make a spotted fur coat. Cruella from Disney's 1961 version of *101 Dalmatians* has a distinctive and memorable appearance due to her bony body, half-black, half-white hair, long red gloves, and large cream fur coat. An alternate version in which Cruella De Vil's cream colored fur coat is replaced by a dalmatian fur coat is remembered by a group of people. The plainness of Cruella's cream fur coat mixed with the strong association between her and dalmatians could reasonably result in a false memory of her wearing a dalmatian fur coat. Her black and white hair might be contributing to the blending of memories involving Cruella's supposed spotted coat and the dalmatians. An intriguing factor to take into consideration is the number of costumes for Cruella De Vil that incorporate dalmatian spots even though they don't accurately reflect the typical appearance used for this character.

The different versions of the coat have an impact on the story since Cruella De Vil's motivation is to make a dalmatian coat. At first glance, it makes sense for Cruella De Vil to not have a spotted coat because it provides a reasonable motivation for her desire to make a spotted coat. However, the alternate version makes sense because she is effortlessly established as an accomplished villain that has likely skinned Dalmatians before. These movies are intended for children, so an over-the-top approach of dressing Cruella De Vil in a spotted coat makes sense. Adults can easily grasp that she wants the dogs for a spotted coat. Cruella's motivation could easily be lost on children since the plain coat does not overtly show her reason for wanting the puppies. The lack of spots on the current version is more likely to diffuse the tension of the movie and potentially confuse young viewers about why the evil lady wants the dalmatians.

Tony the Tiger is the famous feline mascot for *Kellogg's Frosted Flakes*. He first appeared in 1952 and has undergone some design changes over the years. One feature of this cartoon mascot that has seemingly never changed over the years is the color of his nose. Tony's nose has always been blue even though a group of people share a memory of his nose being black. The color of Tony's nose is an easy detail for people to misremember since the color of a cartoon tiger's nose is unlikely to be of high importance in their life. *Family Guy* season 2 episode 14 shows Tony the Tiger with a black nose in a group of breakfast cereal mascots as a parody for *The Breakfast Club. Family Guy* season 5 episode 11 has a parody of Kellogg's mascot known as Terry the Tiger. Interestingly, Terry the Tiger has a blue nose while Tony the Tiger is shown with a black nose.

The Heisman Trophy is an annual award in college football for the most outstanding player as measured by their great ability, diligence, perseverance, and hard work. This prestigious trophy shows a player using the stiff-arm fend with both feet touching the ground and the same design has been used since it was first awarded in 1935. A group of people remember an alternate version of the trophy where the player has one leg lifted in the air. The alternate pose being easier to perform and the high frequency of people lifting their leg for the pose could result in people remembering the trophy's pose incorrectly. One interesting observation is people being photographed striking the alternate pose while holding the actual trophy, such as Barack Obama when he was the Democratic presidential candidate. The tattoo of Micky Mouse doing the Heisman pose on Hines Ward's upper right arm is another possible piece of residue given it demonstrates the alternate version of the pose.

The United States of America is a highly developed country located in North America that is known for economic freedom, quality of life, and military spending. This country has fifty states, a federal district, five major unincorporated territories. There is a significant number of people that remember the United States having fifty-two states even though they are unclear on what the extra two states were. One contributing factor for the possible misremembrance is the line between states and the federal district being blurred due to Washington, D.C. having three votes in the Electoral College. The line is also blurred between states and unincorporated territories because people born in Puerto Rico, Guam, the U.S. Virgin Islands, and the Northern Mariana Islands are considered citizens of the United States. Potential residue for the existence of fifty-two states is found in *Brewster's Millions* when this number of states is mentioned while two lawyers are discussing the extent of Monty's ads for the mayoral election.

The human heart is an important muscular organ that pumps blood to circulate oxygen and nutrients. This critical component of human anatomy is located in the middle of the chest. A significant number of people remember the heart being located on the left side of the chest as evidenced by people being taught the incorrect hand placement for reciting the Pledge of Allegiance of the United States. The beat of the heart is more evident on the left side because it encompasses the strongest pumping chamber of the heart, which is responsible for initiating the blood's circulatory loop. The more perceptible heartbeat on the left side could easily contribute to the idea of the heart itself being located on the left side of the chest. This possible change has a piece of residue involving the biology teacher in *Dead Like Me* season 2 episode 9 explicitly telling her class that the heart is not located in the center of the body.

The Karate Kid is a 1984 film in which a teenage boy named Daniel LaRusso learns karate and life lessons from an Okinawan immigrant named Mr. Miyagi. The current version of the movie shows Daniel LaRusso wearing an iconic white headband with a blue lotus pattern. The headband has seemingly changed from a white headband with a red rising sun design according to a shared memory. This shared memory could originate from the red circle on the flag of Japan and Japan being called the "Land of the Rising Sun." This connection also makes sense considering that Okinawan karate influenced the martial arts seen in the film. One possible piece of residue is found in *Kickin' It Old Skool*, in which Justin Schumacher is tricked into a humorous montage of chores shortly after getting out of a coma. Justin wears a headband with a red rising sun and specifically likens the idea of recovery through the use of chores to Daniel LaRusso's training.

Traffic lights are signals used to control traffic at appropriate locations along roadways and are seen by many people each day. Stoplights have a universal color code in which the red light stops traffic from proceeding, yellow signifies there is an imminent red light, and green means to proceed normally. The configuration in which these lights appear is also consistent with red being at the top, yellow in the middle, and green at the bottom. Traffic lights having green at the top, yellow in the middle, and red at the bottom is remembered by a group of people. One possible reason for this shared memory of a different configuration is the green light being above the red light for railroad signals. *The Simpsons* season 17 episode 7 shows a traffic light with the alternate configuration during a scene in which Marge laments her lack of friends. This is an odd mistake to make considering the consistency of the current configuration.

Charles Lindbergh Jr is commonly known as "the Lindbergh baby" due to his kidnapping and death at 20 months old in 1932. This tragic incident resulted in the "trial of the century", which is strange since there is a widely shared memory of the Lindbergh baby never being found. If memory is to blame, then the common knowledge of the Lindbergh baby kidnapping somehow became disconnected from the massively well-known trial for his death. However, this disconnect between the facts of the kidnapping and the trial is not impossible considering how long ago this incident happened. There are a plethora of references and examples of the alternate memory including a scene from *The Simpsons* season 7 episode 8 in which Grampa Simpson tells the FBI that he is the Lindbergh baby. *Sam & Max Beyond Time and Space* is a video game in which two freelance police officers from modern times find Charles Lindbergh as a talking infant due to the fountain of youth.

Wendy's is currently the third-largest hamburger fast-food chain with over 6,700 locations and is known for its square hamburger patties, the Frosty, and use of fresh ground beef. The company has a well-known corporate logo featuring the founder's daughter with her straight, red hair in pigtails. This corporate logo seems to have changed according to a group of people remembering the girl as having braided hair in pigtails. The alternate version is plausibly explained by misremembrance by blending Wendy's mascot with the appearance of Pippi Longstocking, who has braided red hair sticking out sideways from her head. It is also easy to conflate pigtails and braids since they pair well together and are not very different in appearance when people are not paying close attention. One of the more compelling pieces of possible residue is seen in a Wendy's commercial from 2007 titled Hole in which the featured character wears a redhaired wig with obvious braids.

Zero is Jack Skellington's ghost dog in *The Nightmare Before Christmas* and accompanies his owner on some of his escapades. Zero has a glowing pumpkin nose that perfectly fits the theme of Halloween land. His bright nose comes in handy while leading the sleigh and skeleton reindeer through the foggy skies on Christmas Eve. The glowing pumpkin nose being quite evident throughout the movie comes as a surprise to people sharing a memory of his nose being red without a jack-o-lantern face. This alternate memory is understandable since the difference between red and orange is not as noticeable when considering the size of a dog's nose.

Also, the use of Zero as a replacement for Rudolf can conceivably lead to conflating colors. Interestingly, Zero is depicted as having a red nose in the hardcover version of *The Nightmare Before Christmas* that was published by Golden Books and Disney. It is more difficult to blame this potential oversight on the quality of VHS tapes given the book was released in 2021.

The Jungle Book is a Disney film from 1967 in which a young boy named Mowgli is raised by wolves and befriended by other animals such as the sloth bear named Baloo. One of the most memorable moments of the movie involves Baloo infiltrating a group of monkeys to save Mowgli by disguising himself in a grass skirt along with coconut lips. A group of people remember King Louie being tricked into thinking Baloo was a female using a coconut bra instead of coconut pieces being used as lips. Both disguises are equally ridiculous, so it seems silly to base an actual argument around how convincing a cartoon disguise is. It is possible conflation has occurred due to coconut bras and grass skirts being worn in Hawaii along with the environment of these islands being similar to the setting of the movie. An interesting piece of possible residue is Baloo from Disney's *Once Upon a Dream Parade* having a coconut bra even though he seemingly never wore it in the movie.

CHAPTER 4

MANDELA SUBTRACTIONS

THE THIRD TYPE of quantum change is a Mandela subtraction, which is characterized by the disappearance of a distinguishing feature, phrase, or entity. The existence of this type of change is surprising considering they maintain the specificity and vivid memories associated with the other two types of Mandela effects. Examples for subtractions are not as likely to be caused by a group of people filling in memory gaps because there should be no gap to fill in if the remembered aspect never existed.

It is also difficult to conflate two aspects when one of the aspects is seemingly nonexistent according to reality. Therefore, it is more difficult to give false memories the benefit of the doubt when dealing with

Mandela subtractions. Finding residue for an aspect that has seemingly never existed provides more impactful evidence for a potential change. The balance of power between those purporting misremembrance and those believing a change has occurred is lopsided in favor of the latter group. So, they should consider using subtractions when demonstrating the plausibility of changes.

Star Trek: The Original Series is a science-fiction television show starring William Shatner as Captain James T. Kirk. One of the most iconic lines used by Captain Kirk was remembered and repeated as 'Beam me up, Scotty!' However, this line was never used in any of the episodes of this series or in the movies. This could be due to confabulation and/or people misquoting other phrases such as "Scotty, beam us up", "Scotty, beam me up" and "beam me up".

It might just be a case of the wrong version being repeated so many times that people forget or don't know "Beam me up, Scotty!" wasn't a phrase used by Captain Kirk. The popularity of this apparent misquote might also be why James Doohan, who played Scotty, used it as the title of his autobiography. It is somewhat unusual for an actor to perpetuate a popular misquote connected to his character by naming his autobiography in this manner, so it could be residue of a change.

Richard Simmons is known for his exercise routines in which his infectious energetic personality pairs well with the upbeat music to create approachable 1980s style workout sessions. A prominent feature a group of people remember being associated with Richard Simmons is a headband that he regularly wore during his workout sessions. However, the headband that people remember him wearing does not exist in any of his numerous videos or pictures. The misremembrance of Richard Simmons wearing a headband is not a major leap considering his sweat-inducing fitness routines such as the aptly named videos called *Sweatin' to the Oldies*.

It is interesting how effective the distinguishing headband is for conveying his image through parodies and costumes since he didn't wear it. One such parody is found in the *Rocko's Modern Life* episode titled "No Pain, No Gain", in which Richard Simmons voices an aerobics instructor. This example is intriguing because they managed to get this detail incorrect even though they were directly working with the person they were parodying.

Fruit of the Loom is an American company known for manufacturing clothing such as T-shirts and underwear. This company has a widely recognized logo with a red apple, green grapes, purple grapes, gooseberries, and green leaves. You might wonder why the cornucopia was omitted from the logo's description if you are one of the people remembering a version of the logo that has seemingly never existed. It is possible this alternate memory is conflating the grouping of fruit in this logo with the assortment of food seen spilling out of cornucopias around the months of Autumn. The underwear logo seen in *South Park* season 16 episode 6 might hold a piece of residue since it says "Cornucopia Brand" and has a banana and grapes in front of a cornucopia. This is an interesting choice since the fruit is likely to remind people of Fruit of the Loom while including a cornucopia in the name and picture misses the mark.

Shared memories of the Fruit of the Loom logo including a cornucopia provides an important perspective for this phenomenon.

The shared misconception of a cornucopia being called a loom due to limited vocabulary skills is an important perspective to consider when determining the soundness of some Mandela changes being caused by false memories. On one hand, the common outcome of people mistakenly thinking a cornucopia is called a loom due to shared context clues is positive reinforcement for people thinking and storing memories in similar ways.

For example, fruit is shown in the logo and mentioned in the brand name, so it understandable for people to collectively correlate the cornucopia with the last word in the brand name. On the other hand, these shared experiences of correlating images and words is problematic from the perspective of misremembrance since the cornucopia was never on the logo. These people somehow came to the same flawed conclusion using the cornucopia as a reference point even though none of them actually saw a cornucopia at the time of making the correlation if a change hasn't happened.

Moonraker is the eleventh movie in the James Bond franchise with Richard Kiel's reprised role as the seemingly indestructible henchman with sharp steel teeth. Richard Kiel's character is aptly named "Jaws" and the movie has a memorable scene where he meets Blanche Ravalec's character named "Dolly" and they fall in love. A group of people have a shared memory in which Dolly smiles at Jaws and this reveals braces on her teeth. This memory does not match reality because she does not have braces. Dolly having braces when they fall in love at first sight makes sense given the metal on Jaw's teeth, so a perceived memory gap might have been filled in by a group of people.

A possible piece of residue involves a Finnish commercial for the Sampo Mini Visa Card in which the scene from Moonraker is parodied. Richard Kiel is in the commercial and he gives the cashier a big smile followed by her smiling and revealing her braces.

Jaws and Dolly falling in love is a strange scene to include in the movie considering Dolly does not have braces. Notably, it is unusual for a villain to have the start of their romantic relationship explored during a movie's runtime, but the filmmakers obviously felt it was worthwhile to include. It is plausible that the filmmakers took the time to include the scene of them falling in love because it showcased how even a character like Jaws can find someone with similarities.

This message is obviously lost if Dolly does not have braces because their only similar feature is nonexistent, which results in the scene feeling out of place. Having convincing relationship building is not a strong suit of Bond films, which makes the inclusion of a scene showing this type of development even stranger. They could have easily shown Jaws as already having a girlfriend and nothing meaningful would have been lost or gained since they currently have no obvious focal point driving their instant attraction.

Lassie is a television show that ran for 17 seasons and is known for the lead character of a Rough Collie dog and a boy named Timmy Martin, who was played by Jon Provost. A well-known episode of the show involves Lassie getting help for Timmy after he fell into a well. This is one of the best-known scenes in the show's history even though Timmy never fell into a well during any episode. Instead, it was Lassie who fell into a well during a two-part episode in season 17 called "For the Love of Lassie".

It is possible that a false memory emerged

about Timmy falling in a well given how many other places he fell into such as rivers, lakes, quicksand, and an abandoned mineshaft. It is incredible how many parodies and references exist for this memorable scenario that never existed. One of the most interesting pieces of potential residue is the memoir titled *Timmy's in the Well: The Jon Provost Story*.

I Love Lucy is a television sitcom that originally aired from 1951 to 1957 and was the most-watched show in the United States for more than half of this time. The show focuses on the life of Lucy and Ricky Ricardo and humorously follows Lucy's various failed attempts to get into showbiz. Ricky saying, "Lucy! You got some 'splainin' to do!" is one of the best-known catchphrases from the show even though he never said this in any episode. This potential false memory could be caused by Ricky saying variations of the catchphrase in a similar way to how people remember the alternate version being used. This widely remembered catchphrase that seemingly never existed on the show has somehow been parodied numerous times while the current versions are conspicuously missing. *Fools Rush In* shows one such instance of potential residue where

Alex Whitman uses the seemingly missing line rather than any of the versions that exist in our current reality.

Kellogg's Raisin Bran is a breakfast cereal that uses the slogan "two scoops of raisins in every box" and has an animated sun named "Sunny" as its mascot. Sunny reinforces the company's slogan for the cereal by holding two scoops full of raisins over a bowl filled with Raisin Bran. Sunny seems to be missing a memorable feature according to people with a shared memory of him wearing sunglasses. Some people even remember the sunglasses playing a role in an ad campaign in which sunlight was the secret ingredient used to make their raisins taste good. A possible source for conflation is the sunglasses worn by The California Raisins, which were popular around the time people have vivid memories of Sunny wearing sunglasses in commercials. A parody of Sunny is seen dropping giant raisins out of two scoops in *Family Guy* season 1 episode 2. One feature in this parody that does not make sense based on our current reality is the inclusion of glasses.

The 1995 adaptation of *Pride and Prejudice* is a British television series starring Colin

Firth as Mr. Darcy and Jennifer Ehle as Elizabeth Bennet. The original series was watched by over 10 million people and had an overwhelmingly positive response from critics. The lake scene where Mr. Darcy is seen walking out of a lake with his shirt clinging to him was determined to be one of the most memorable moments in British television history. This scene somehow became one of the most memorable television moments even though it never happened according to all evidence from the actual show. There are only scenes of Mr. Darcy entering the lake, swimming, and walking away from the lake while his heartthrob exit from the lake is distinctly missing. It is possible these people filled in this perceived gap of Mr. Darcy exiting the lake by splicing the other scenes together. Strangely, a variety of shows and movies have made tributes to this scene even though it apparently never existed.

The Twilight Zone is an anthology television series created by Rod Serling, which has had a wide appeal thanks to the variety of genres involved and unexpected twists. A group of people remember many if not all episodes of the show starting with Rod Serling saying, "Imagine if you will…" This line is inextricably linked to Rod Serling and *The Twilight Zone* even though he never started a single episode with this phrase. The residue is absolutely staggering for the supposed existence of this memorable phrase including memes, articles falsely attributing the phrase, and Futurama parodying it through *The Scary Door* referencing the nonexistent line.

Rod Serling and *The Twilight Zone* are both typically mentioned by name when an article or person 'borrows' this useful introduction. The believability that a change happened with this line boils down to how likely so many people would point out the origins of the phrase incorrectly. What is even weirder is there seems to be no source for the possible conflation of this line.

Monopoly is a popular board game based around buying properties and bankrupting opponents through rents and trading. The game's mascot is fittingly a wealthy old man with a white mustache, morning suit, and black top hat who is known as "Rich Uncle Pennybags", "Mr. Monopoly" and/or "The Monopoly Man". The memorable feature that seems to be missing from Rich Uncle Pennybags is a monocle over his left eye according to a shared memory. A possible source for confabulation is the monocle worn by the mascot of Planters known as Mr. Peanut since they both use a cane and wear a top hat. *Ace Ventura: Pet Detective* has an interesting piece of potential residue in the form of a scene in which Jim Carrey's character says to an older man, "And you must be the Monopoly guy!" This comparison is intriguing since the man has a monocle, but lacks other distinguishing features associated with Rich Uncle Pennybags such as a cane and top hat.

Curious George is a chimpanzee, well-known for the mischief he gets into during his adventures chronicled in a series of books, a television series, and movies. The husband-and-wife team consisted of Margret Rey as the writer and Hans Augusto "H. A." Rey as the illustrator. Their choice to not include a tail not only lets us know he is a chimpanzee but is also the focus of this Mandela subtraction since a group of people remember him having a tail.

George is referred to as a monkey on numerous occasions throughout the character's history, so it is not farfetched for people to remember him as a monkey rather than a chimpanzee. Also, the line between chimpanzee and monkey is blurred for some people because "monkey" is a catch-all term used for various species of primates. These factors could feasibly lead to people remembering Curious George as having a tail since most species of monkeys are known to have one.

Curious George made his debut as a character near the onset of World War II while Margret and H. A. Rey lived in France. Curious George was actually called "Zozo" in the United Kingdom around this time, which was likely to avoid using King George VI's name for a monkey. This deviation in George's name is advantageous in terms of locating possible residue for his tail. H.A. Rey illustrated a series of cartoons featuring "Zozo" for *Good Housekeeping Magazine,* in which the character clearly has a tail. It makes sense the name "Zozo" was used since the magazine was also published in the United Kingdom at this point. These six panel comic strips showed various instances of George getting into mischief such as blowing up a firework in an office. One such comic strip used "Zozo" as the header and shows Curious George spinning around fast on a record player. This particular example is a color pencil illustration by

H.A. Rey that appeared in a 1951 issue of *Good Housekeeping Magazine.*

Risky Business is a well-known film from 1983 starring Tom Cruise in his breakout role as Joel Goodson. One of the first things Joel did with the house to himself was dance in his underwear and shirt while the song "Old Time Rock and Roll" was playing in the background. One memorable aspect of this scene is missing according to the shared memory of Tom Cruise wearing Ray-Ban sunglasses while sliding across the floor and spinning around. People misremembering Cruise's character wearing the famous Ray-Bans during the iconic dance scene is not out of the question considering they are featured on the movie poster and worn by Joel in other scenes of the movie. There are numerous recreations of this dance scene that include sunglasses such as *The Goldbergs* season 3 episode 1. There is less ambiguity about where the inspiration came from for Barry Goldberg's attempts at sliding across the floor in his underwear given the episode was heavily influenced by *Risky Business.*

Shazaam is a film from the early to mid-90s where Sinbad plays a genie. The only problem is that this seems to be a shared false memory since Sinbad claims he never starred in the movie and the movie seemingly never existed. A troubling part of this shared memory is the plot was apparently so generic and unmemorable that people struggle to remember many details. The unmemorable storyline and dialogue are also difficult to reproduce given that these memories are from supposedly watching the movie decades ago. The *Sinbad the Sailor* movie marathon in 1994 was hosted by none other than Sinbad dressed in a genie costume, which could support residue or confabulation. On one hand, he could have dressed like a genie while hosting the marathon to promote the movie *Shazaam*. On the other hand, Sinbad being dressed as a genie during the marathon could be an important piece of the puzzle for the emergence of shared memories that combined into a movie called *Shazaam*.

Sinbad was actively making movies during this time period and the supposed movie called *Shazaam* is something he plausibly would have starred in. People are confident that they are not confusing *Shazaam* with *Kazaam*, which is a 1996 genie movie starring Shaquille O'Neal. People vividly remember *Kazaam* as being a blatant knockoff of *Shazaam* even though the latter never existed. A compelling piece of possible residue is seen in *All That* season 2 episode 13, in which Sinbad's character says, "I am Sinboo." This line is reminiscent of Sinbad saying "I am Shazaam" in *Shazaam* and Shaq saying "I am Kazaam" in *Kazaam*.

However, the former movie seemingly never existed, and the latter released months after this episode aired. Another possible reference to the nonexistent movie is Sinboo holding his arms in positions reminiscent of other genies such as the one in *Kazaam*. The smoke used as Sinboo entered the room might also have been a reference to Sinbad's genie coming out of a lamp.

Britney Spears is a singer, songwriter, and dancer and one of the world's best-selling music artists with over 100 million records sold worldwide. Her album *Oops!... I Did It Again* peaked at number one on the US Billboard 200 and sold over 1.3 million copies in its first week. "Oops!... I Did It Again" was the lead single for this album and had its own music video in which Britney wore a memorable red PVC bodysuit. The microphone headset some people remember her wearing during this music video has apparently disappeared. A plausible source for this possible misremembrance is the fact Britney Spears wore a microphone headset at other times such as during live performances. Lizzie McGuire season 1 episode 2 has potential residue for the remembered headset since Hilary Duff's character imagines herself as Britney Spears from the "Oops!... I Did It Again" music video. Lizzie McGuire wore the remembered headset along with the red suit while her animated alter-ego wore a headset without the red suit.

The Matrix is a science fiction action movie from 1999 that explores the idea of people not knowing they live in a simulation and stars Keanu Reeves as Neo and Laurence Fishburne as Morpheus. When Neo meets Morpheus for the first time some people remember Morpheus saying, "What if I told you…" before confirming the Matrix is real. It is unlikely to be a misquote since nothing has replaced the seemingly missing line and other lines from the movie are not similar. The movie came out well before memes became popular, so it is not inconceivable for people creating the original Morpheus memes in 2012 to use something that was not actually said.

These meme creators taking creative liberties could have planted a false memory of Morpheus saying the line. However, this does not explain why Morpheus says, "What if I were to tell you that you are seeing the world the way it actually is" in *South Park* season 11 episode 11. This episode airing in 2007 means it could be residue for a change since it predates the earliest Morpheus memes by over four years.

This memorable line from *The Matrix* apparently disappearing is what made me realize there might be something going on beyond confabulation. I wondered if I could have possibly made up this line that I could vividly recreate in my memory after watching the movie so many times. If I had made it up, then how did so many other people make up this exact same line in their own memories? I would have accepted misremembrance if the line was slightly altered, but I could not realistically accept so many people misremembering such an iconic line if the line never existed.

I then spent a couple of years thinking about whether time travel, parallel universes, or a simulation would best explain the Mandela effect. Any credibility of time travel being involved went out the window because residue would be impossible with this explanation. The idea of parallel universes took much longer to dismiss on a personal level and was accomplished through various thought experiments based around the double slit experiment.

Dismissing these alternatives left the possibility of a simulation or an immense number of coincidences centered on the exact same trivial aspects. The idea of coincidences seemed ludicrous given the specificity involved with people misremembering the exact same aspects in the exact same way even though some of these aspects seemingly never existed. No degree of bad memory was going to feasibly explain away this line disappearing or other Mandela subtractions, so it was time to think about which other possible explanation was most plausible.

I also knew my limits on what is acceptable as a believable coincidence after writing a book about purposeful evolution. The idea of Mandela subtractions being a coincidence would have been more acceptable if it was a one-off occurrence. However, even a one-off occurrence that is convincing enough brings the validity of misremembrance into question. It is quite fitting that a missing line from *The Matrix* is what led me down the path of wondering if we actually live in a simulation.

CHAPTER 5
SIMULATION THEORY

THE EXPLANATION I propose for the emergence of Mandela substitutions, shifts, and subtractions involves our collective experiences in reality being part of a hyper realistic simulation. This possibility seems to be the best explanation for the existence of residue because a convincing virtual reality might have imperfections that can become apparent to those within the simulation. The advantage of residue over other potential inconsistencies within a simulation is the relative newness of noticing its emergence even though changes are spread retroactively.

This allows us to focus on relatively new developments that could cause the emergence of Mandela effects while other potential inconsistencies within a simulation would be extremely difficult to explore in a similar manner. This chapter focuses on why Mandela changes might emerge within a simulation rather than other topics such as why the simulation exists. The following proposed limitations of a hypothetical virtual reality have some potential for explaining why this phenomenon started emerging relatively recently.

It is difficult for people to recognize when they have a false memory as has been shown in various studies. However, people can recognize something as a false memory if evidence is found that contradicts the influenced memory. It would be even more difficult to recognize a memory that has been overwritten within a simulation since reality would typically change to match this new memory. If memories of some people were properly overwritten to match the new reality and others retained the original memory of an aspect, then something similar to the Mandela effect could occur. The people with the improperly overwritten memory could choose to overlook this minor inconsistency as they know their own memory is not perfect. Those in the second group could also choose to believe a change has occurred and come up with theories for how reality changed. The members of the latter group exploring reasons for alternate memories would rightly be looked at as odd given they are trusting memories that don't match reality.

The emergence of Mandela changes is reliant on the idea of the simulation being run on a system that does not have access to a vast number of resources. This is important to consider because a vast number of resources would be needed to fully load every particle in our universe if it part of a simulation. It would make sense to cut corners for resource requirements through methods of efficiency such as illusions if the available resources are limited. If the system has access to unlimited resources, then it would be highly unlikely for noticeable discrepancies caused by straining the system to emerge within the simulation.

Therefore, my idea of the system's limited access to resources allowing glitches to occur would be impossible if this limitation does not exist. These limitations also assume the system is based on pragmatic principles so that the system is only provided with enough resources for the simulation to continue running as intended. If there are limits to the number of available resources, then there could be consequences when these limits are surpassed.

An indication that we live in a virtual reality run by an efficient system is the perpetual existence of superposition when a recorded measurement has not occurred. Having variables represented by a range of possible outcomes is likely less resource intensive than maintaining defined states for each particle. Having approximations for variables instead of defined characteristics is useful because the former requires the equivalent of a question mark, while the latter requires specific attributes to be maintained, stored, and altered as changes occur.

There is no question about whether superposition exists as the double slit experiment clearly proves this state of being is part of our reality. An important question is whether superposition would exist in a system with access to a vast number of resources such as sufficient computing power. The use of superposition within a simulation would make a lot of sense if there were a lack of resources for loading the staggering amount of information our universe would require otherwise.

The collapse of wave functions would be a useful last-ditch effort to convince people their reality is not a simulation. Particles being in a perpetual existence of superposition has seemingly not had negative consequences over the span of billions of years. This means a particle's ability to stop being in a state of superposition when a recorded measurement occurs is peculiar in the grand scheme of things.

For instance, particles interact with each other according to the laws of physics whether their wave functions have collapsed or not. The only difference between the wave function collapse and superposition appears to be the information gained through a recorded measurement. It would be a huge red flag if recorded measurements did not generate defined data because it would indicate a lack of defined variables at the quantum level. Therefore, the benefit of allowing particles to have a defined state would likely be of higher importance than the benefits of keeping the particle in superposition. Making the quantum level function like the macro level when a recorded measurement happens is useful for maintaining the illusion of particles being defined objects rather than revealing their probabilistic nature.

The existence of wave function collapses is problematic given how it seems to serve no practical purpose within the universe. Additionally, there seems to be only one way to achieve a truly collapsed wave function and that is through a recorded measurement. The ability to have collapsed wave functions would make sense if this was required for a functioning universe. If particles needed to achieve decoherence to properly interact with other particles for the formation of galaxies, then recorded measurements needed to happen at the beginning of the universe. If recorded measurements were not required for the universe to form, then why do wave functions act differently now in comparison to that point in time? This is the type of inconsistency that arises if decoherence was accomplished in the past without recorded measurements while this requirement currently exists for the collapse of wave functions. The universe has apparently been able to function properly for billions of years while particles perpetually existed in superposition. This points to a lack of explanatory power for the ability to achieve a truly collapsed wave function.

The explanatory power of multiple universes existing due to collapsing wave functions loses its strength if superposition has been the default state of the universe for billions of years. If multiple outcomes from a wave function collapse don't exist without a recorded measurement, then the mechanism for forming parallel universes has only been operational for a relatively short period of time. This would drastically reduce the number of parallel universes, given that experiments making measurements at the quantum level might be the only way this type of collapse happens.

This is problematic because it turns the formation of parallel universes from being overwhelmingly common to being impossible, until relatively recently. The explanatory power of parallel universes in terms of the Mandela effect would be lost because some changes seem to have retroactively affected points in history predating our first recorded measurements at the quantum level. If branching was not possible at a certain point in history, then it is highly unlikely parallel universes were involved in potential changes dating back that far.

If parallel universes have been branching regardless of whether a wave function truly collapsed, then a method reliant on this type of wave function collapse likely loses all explanatory power. This type of branching would involve every outcome of each wave function happening in a separate universe at any given moment without superposition being disrupted. There would need to be an explanation for the existence of a difference between a truly collapsed wave function and the perpetual wave function collapses that don't disrupt superposition.

Otherwise, there is no explanatory power for the different outcomes seen during the double slit experiment because there would essentially be no difference between the two scenarios. This is because every branching possibility would happen whether a recorded measurement occurred or not. The existence of a difference between these two scenarios means this type of branching is unlikely to have any explanatory power in terms of physics or Mandela changes. An alternative is to explain why particles remain in superposition after a wave function collapses rather than each particle maintaining the defined outcome they have in accordance to the newly branched parallel universes.

The simulation's usage of resources could be reduced even further if superposition is not a sufficient way of achieving desired efficiency levels. One such method is projecting realistic illusions for other sections of the universe so that not even particles in superposition need to be maintained. This would be an effective way of conserving resources since we lack the means of physically scrutinizing these faraway sections of the universe.

The implementation of this type of illusion could be accomplished using holographic technology. An accurate illusion at great distances has the benefit of greatly reduced resource costs while not breaking the immersion of the simulation. Our models for cosmic events function without accounting for every particle that would be involved, so it is plausible for advanced recreations of sections of the universe to exist within a hyper realistic simulation. The system having more methods of efficiency built in would also help explain the emergence of

Mandela changes because it further alludes to the system having limitations that can potentially be surpassed.

A way in which the system might use more resources than intended is generating information during recorded measurements. Generating this previously undefined information uses resources at a higher rate for a period of time. There would also likely be an uptick in resource consumption for the maintenance of previously generated information. This drain on resources decreases after the information has been generated and the new data has entered a maintenance mode. The drain of resources would be proportional to the amount of information being generated during a given period of time.

For instance, the collapse of a wave function due to measuring the which-way information of a single particle is going to be less draining on the system than simultaneously measuring attributes of multiple particles. This drain of resources might be mitigated by borrowing from other processes within the simulation until the information has entered maintenance mode. This could be a problem in terms of available resources for other important processes within the simulation when a lot of information is generated through recorded measurements.

CERN (the European Organization for Nuclear Research) is known for its research using The Large Hadron Collider (LHC) to record results from the collision of accelerated particles. This type of experiment at the quantum level is likely to cause the simulation to use an increased number of resources if results from these recorded measurements are generated simultaneously. The sheer number of impacts would likely overwhelm the simulation even more if triggers were not used to reduce the amount of gathered information.

The emergence of Mandela effects also eerily coincides with the operating schedule of the LHC. For example, Fiona Broome attended the conference where she found others shared her memory of Mandela's death happening in the 1980s in the same year that the LHC started performing collisions. However, the retroactive nature of quantum changes makes it difficult to accurately determine when a potential change actually emerged. It is not as difficult to recognize the connection or coincidence of spikes in the discovery of Mandela changes in comparison to the run dates of the LHC. There also seems to be a connection or coincidental positive correlation between the noteworthiness of Mandela effects that emerge, and the amount of data collected by CERN's particle experiments.

The importance of resource limitations and strain on the system through generating recorded information is the resultant glitches that might happen. Glitches that alter or delete aspects within the simulation would typically be prevented if sufficient resources are available.

A time during which there might not be sufficient resources for maintaining corrective measures is when resources are diverted to other functions within the system such as when definite information for particles is generated. It would not be surprising if a significant number of resources are diverted from other functions during LHC experiments given that around 140 terabytes of data is generated in a single day of operation. The apparent spikes in the emergence of Mandela changes during periods of experiments done with the LHC is an important indicator of this type of resource diversion. This is an important indicator because these types of spikes should not occur if these alternate memories are the byproduct of confabulation. Instead, there should be a distinct lack of correlation to events such as run dates of the LHC if false memories are involved because these would likely emerge sporadically.

Residue of the original version might exist because the glitches causing changes within the simulation are not able to recognize abstract copies of an aspect. This is especially true for instances in which the copy is used in creative ways that are not explicitly related to the original content such as memes and parodies. Therefore, the accuracy for glitches overwriting aspects within the simulation is directly tied to the number of similarities between the original content and a copy of this aspect.

For example, a person standing next to *The Thinker* while performing the original pose is not going to be easily recognized by the overwriting process. The person is not closely connected to the statue even while doing a similar pose. In contrast, it is difficult to find residue for Mandela substitutions because the changes are too small for people to likely differentiate a copy to a sufficient degree for the glitch to overlook it. Finding copies of an aspect that are obscure enough to avoid the detection of glitches is likely a good way of distinguishing between a group experiencing a Mandela change and a false memory.

The complexity involved with interrelated memories combined with a lack of resources and/or overwriting accuracy likely explains the discrepancy in people having memories of the current version versus the alternate version. This would explain why every person is affected by an undeterminable set of Mandela changes. This is further complicated by the potential ability of people experiencing cognitive dissonance caused by glitches to alter memories in an attempt to remove inconsistencies in their memory.

On the sone hand, this might happen if the person can't handle the idea of an aspect changing and their brain overwrites examples of the alternate memory to protect them from this inconsistency. On the other hand, people could trust their original memory so much that their brain overwrites instances of conflicting memories even though these alternate memories don't match reality. This attempt at consistency within the brain might be similar to how the brain fills in memory gaps with plausible substitutions rather than leaving a gap. Groups of people having shared memories of the current or alternate version is a fascinating topic that needs further research to understand it better.

There is likely a higher priority for overwriting the alternate version of an aspect based on how closely connected a person is to the aspect that has changed. One possible explanation is the cognitive dissonance is much stronger if a direct connection exists.

For example, if an organ has changed locations, then a person with a background in the medical field is going to experience a heightened sense of cognitive dissonance in response to the change. The heightened sense of cognitive dissonance would greatly increase the likelihood of memories tied to the alternate version being overwritten by memories of the current version. This would also explain why people from South Africa were not shocked by Nelson Mandela becoming president in 1994 since they would not have the shared memory of his death. If

Mandela died in the 1980s before a Mandela change occurred, then there was a priority for overwriting the memory of the death for people living in the country.

The trivial nature of Mandela effects is likely the reason these changes have not been manually fixed. There have likely been changes we don't know about that were manually changed because their noticeability was too high. Otherwise, it seems like too much of a coincidence that most Mandela changes have involved trivial aspects. The more noticeable changes would be worth pausing and/or rewinding the simulation while a major change and consequences tied to the change are fixed.

In contrast, the minor changes that can be rationalized away through confabulation would not be as much of a priority to manually fix. It would likely not be worth the cost in time and resources to fix an aspect if a change is not noticeable enough to directly break immersion within the simulation. However, this is also a risky stance to take because a multitude of small changes can potentially cause a disturbance equivalent to a major change, which ultimately breaks immersion within the simulation.

CHAPTER 6
CONCLUSION

MY FIRST PREDICTION based on past data such as run dates for the LHC is another spike in the emergence of Mandela effects during future periods of activity for similar experiments. The number of emerging Mandela effects should increase in direct proportion to the increase in data collected during these time periods. For example, the amount of data collected during future runs for the LCH, and its successor(s), will likely increase dramatically, so the number of noticeable Mandela changes should increase accordingly.

The moderation of changes will likely continue, so rationalization will continue to be a factor regardless of how many quantum changes emerge during a given time period.

However, it will become more difficult to attribute changes to misremembrance, provided an appreciable increase does in fact happen during these time periods as I predict. There might also be a small uptick in the emergence of Mandela effects between run times because there is likely a gradual increase in resources necessary for the maintenance mode of so much information. These increases will hopefully be offset by an influx of additional resources, but there should still be spikes according to the emergent pattern.

My second prediction is that Mandela changes will also become more pronounced as the amount of information gathered by these types of experiments increases. The immersion of breaking Mandela changes will likely still be manually fixed, but the ones that are not fixed should become more noteworthy as the number of diverted resources increases.

If my prediction is correct, then the changes will become more noteworthy as experiments gather more and more information and it will become increasingly difficult to write the changes off as faulty memory. If the tolerance level for allowing the persistence of changes is at a degree that allows subtractions such as *Shazaam,* then further changes of this magnitude could occur during future spikes.

Noticeability will likely be somewhat mitigated by the distribution of each type of quantum change since substitutions will still be more numerous than subtractions with shifts having a frequency between the other two. This buffer to noticeability is because Mandela substitutions are much easier to rationalize away than subtractions. The proportion of each type of Mandela change in relation to the overall number of Mandela effects that emerge during each spike will likely remain steady.

The possible revelation that we exist in a simulation should not matter for our experiences within our reality. Would you actually make different choices in your life if you knew the universe was simulated? I don't think people would act any differently because there are still positive and negative consequences whether we are in a simulation or not. People can live their lives and pursue what they find meaningful regardless of the underlying foundation of reality.

This continues to be a reality based on

causality and provides opportunities for an experience that are preferable to nonexistence even if we do happen to exist in a simulation. I would argue that even the worst experience within a simulated reality would be preferable to not having an opportunity to exist. This is because most people have at least some positive experiences in their lifetime even though there is a lot of pain and misery in this reality.

Lastly, the level of meaning a person attributes to an aspect within this reality should realistically not change just because the true foundation of this reality might not be what they thought it was.

Printed in Great Britain
by Amazon

24107775R00061